YOUR KNOWLEDGE HAS VALUE

- We will publish your bachelor's and master's thesis, essays and papers

- Your own eBook and book - sold worldwide in all relevant shops

- Earn money with each sale

Upload your text at www.GRIN.com
and publish for free

Bibliographic information published by the German National Library:

The German National Library lists this publication in the National Bibliography; detailed bibliographic data are available on the Internet at http://dnb.dnb.de .

This book is copyright material and must not be copied, reproduced, transferred, distributed, leased, licensed or publicly performed or used in any way except as specifically permitted in writing by the publishers, as allowed under the terms and conditions under which it was purchased or as strictly permitted by applicable copyright law. Any unauthorized distribution or use of this text may be a direct infringement of the author s and publisher s rights and those responsible may be liable in law accordingly.

Imprint:

Copyright © 2017 GRIN Verlag
Print and binding: Books on Demand GmbH, Norderstedt Germany
ISBN: 9783668738607

This book at GRIN:

https://www.grin.com/document/429922

Anqi Liu

Postcolonial Identity and Place

"Who am I?"

GRIN Verlag

GRIN - Your knowledge has value

Since its foundation in 1998, GRIN has specialized in publishing academic texts by students, college teachers and other academics as e-book and printed book. The website www.grin.com is an ideal platform for presenting term papers, final papers, scientific essays, dissertations and specialist books.

Visit us on the internet:

http://www.grin.com/

http://www.facebook.com/grincom

http://www.twitter.com/grin_com

Hausarbeit:
Postcolonial Identity and Place

Contents

1. Introduction 2

2. Identity: How to treat yourself 3

2.1 Grey Owl: A reasonable escape and the search for true-self 4

3 Place: Where should I belong? 6

3.1 Isabelle Eberhardt: Even the clearest mirror loses its function 7

4. Grey Owl and Isabelle Eberhardt: A Comparison 8

5. Conclusion 9

References 10

1. Introduction

Postcolonialism is the continual shedding of the old skin of Western thought and discourse and the emergence of new self-awareness, critique, and celebration. It is like a process of Lost and Found. Their lands were conquered, the sense of displacement is strong, but the self-awareness was awakened and transformed into a burning self-expression.

Ashcroft emphasized that " more than three quarters of the people living of the world today have had their lives shaped by the experience of colonialism."[1] This kind of colonial experience threw the colonized countries into dilemma and contradiction. Even if they got independence, they still confused their identity and culture.

What is the right attitude towards the colonialism? Many critics have argued that colonialism is like a cultural disaster which destroyed indigenous cultures, It is a reasonable argument, colonialism was not just a power control, but also a cultural control. A mass of documentaries has showed the tragic life of the indigenous people under the oppression of colonialism. However, this argument underestimates the resilience and adaptability of colonial societies. In my opinion, what the most attractive part of the postcolonialism is the capacity of changes and adaptions. Culture is not a static process, a large number of components determines where the culture moves towards and what the final form of the culture is. In my view, this question is like a multiple choice. The answers may be ambivalent but all the answers are reasonable.

Post-colonial theory involved with broad range of cultural phenomenon, politics, history and military, postcolonial literatures has positioned itself as a key entry point to postcolonial theory. In addition to its own regional characteristics, postconlonial literatures had also the implication of colonized experiences and thoughts. On the basis of it, some characteristics of post-colonial theory would become evident.

Postcolonial studies aim at stripping away conventional thoughts and examine what kind of identity emerges in postcolonial subject. The first problem when I set out to work on postcolonial literatures is to confirm its scope. This word scope that I put forward here can be

---

1. Ashcroft, Bill et al. (1989) The Empire Writes Back: Theory and Practice in post-colonial literatures. London-New York: Routledge

explained as follows, on the one hand, postcolonial literature is apparently vague and general. It's such a multinational and multicultural case that it is hard to define which country falls under the rubric. Except what we always mentioned as "postcolonial countries" such as Nigeria, India and Pakistan, some writers include also countries like Canada, Ireland and Australia. So when we read the literatures about postcolonial, it is apparent for us to discover, that they include two parts, on the one hand, it is based on the dominant or colonizer society, on the other hand, it talks also about the dominated or colonized society.

On the other hand, there are a large number of relevant themes or aspects around the topic postcolonialism: migration, race, gender, resistance, slavery and so on. Trying to cover all the countries and aspects in one essay seems not so specific. In my essay, I will focus on the question "Who am I ?". This kind of doubt about one's identity is a "derivative product" of colonialism and a very important topic in postcolonial world. When we read literatures, we are able to seek out, what the indigenous voice want to express, how should the indigenous people see themselves, once their place and identity were forced to change? Is the dual identity always ambivalent? These questions are what I'm going to explain hereinafter.

2. Identity: How to treat myself

One of a main feature of the postcolonial period lies in the continual focus on the problem of identity, which existed in all postcolonial communities. "Lost and Found" became the main topic of this time. What has been changed and what has been remained during the time of vagabondage? When a wanderer was forced to arrive a new country, his whole worldview may be changed. Such an earthshaking change must have far-reaching effects on self-awareness and autognosis.

> Cultural identities come from somewhere, have histories. But, like everything which is historical, they undergo constant transformation. Far from being eternally fixed in some essentialised past, they are subject to the continuous'play'of history, culture and power. Far from being grounded in mere 'recovery'of the past, which is waiting to be found,

will secure our sense of ourselves into eternity, identities are names we give to the different ways we are positioned by, and position ourselves within the narratives of the past. [2]

(225)

David Hume has ever said: "Of all relations the most universal is that of identity, being common to every being whose existence has any duration." [3] When we refer to the concept "identity", the first word I used to describe this concept is "clear". But in the period of postcolonial, In addition to own their personal identity, people have to know who they are in relation to larger community and face the change of the nation, conquered or being conquered. Mercer has argued "identity only becomes an issue when it is in crisis, when something assumed to be fixed, coherent and stable is displaced by the experience of doubt and uncertainty." In the following case of Grey Owl, I am going to present his double identity and try to explain his ambivalent identities.

2.1 Grey Owl: a reasonable escape and a search of true-self

A white Indian called Grey Owl showed a double and ambivalent identity. The ambiguity of his parentage made it hard for him to find his true-self. In my opinion, when we try to discuss somebody's character, what we must handle in advance is their parentage. It will be the first-hand information. Archie's father was an inveterate wanderer, he traveled to Florida and returned years later to Hastings as a mysterious figure. Archie knows little about his mother. There is an interesting point, both of his parents is mysterious, instead of living an ordinary life, they seems extraordinary, which gave Archie a space of fantasy. He tried to fantasize that his mother was an American Indian and from the perspective of blood relationship, he himself was therefore half Indian. This self-made intriguing belief made him act as a real Indian. This so-called "half- breed" tends to cultural rather than racial.

Smith Rosenberg has ever written: "The colonized other, denied the basic characteristics of

---

[2]. Hall, Stuart. (1990). 'Cultural Identity and Diaspora' in Jonathan Rutherford, *Identity:Community, Culture, Difference*, London:Lawrece and Wishart. P.225.

3 Hume, David. A Treatise of Human Nature: Volume 1:Texts (Clarendon Press, Oxford:2007) , P15.

subjectivity, not only gives up its essence to the colonizer, it is transformed into a dark mirror that reflects and confirms the colonizer's power"[4]

At that time, Grey Owl's Canada consisted of two parts: one the civilized South, home of Europeans, the other, the wild northlands, home of Indians. Grey Owl believed, the relationship between the colonizer and the colonized should not be defined briefly as "occupy and obey", it was not a competition which always had winner or loser. To Grey Owl, It was the North that made Canada unique and precious. The forest and the river provided the people with calmness, which was too much different from the general background of colonization and occupation. To him, one can try to integrate into the life in the North or just destroy it, but no way to win it. Instead of conquering, people went to North to survive, to discover the real-self, and that was what he did. This dual identity of civilized and savage which he envisioned for Canada also formed part of his own being. In the dualism of Indian and white, he referred to identify himself with the former.

I came up with an new idea, There was a game called transpositional consideration, it means that thinking something in another state, so I just made an assumption, if he was born as an Indian and lived in wilderness, he would also have the longing for the life as an white man and pursued the western culture. So this is an ambivalent situation. People might always want what they can't get. Looking at the background of Archie's life, we can draw a conclusion, that he tried to flee from his hopeless life in western country, he chose to live like a primitive man, who only take manual labour and don't need to think too much, don't need to face the pressure of study, social communication, job etc. What I want to say here is that, this escapism made the second identity of Archie.

When he owned these double identities, "escapism" would no longer became a word to describe him. As a white Canadian named Archie Belaney, he became a pioneer conservationist and intended to "arouse in the Canadian people a sense of responsibility they have for the north country and its inhabitants, humans and animal"[5]. As an Indian called Grey Owl, he tried to redeem the image of the Indians, instead of being depressingly drunk, dirty and hapless, he wanted to demonstrate that, Indians could also hold themselves with dignity

---

[4] Smith-Rosenberg, Carroll. (2010). This Violent Empire – The Birth Of An American National Identity. The University Of North Carolina Press, America, P 202
[5] http://canadianicon.org/table-of-contents/grey-owl-white-indian/

and belief. This masquerade was more than a racial idea within the identity and writings of Grey Owl, it is also for the space and environment that he tried to save and protect. I have mentioned a word "ambivalent" to describe his dual – identity, but now I found, this kind of "ambivalent" can be transformed into a harmonious aim. His endeavor and work are intended to present a need to incorporate the past and then influence the modern life. As I mentioned before, instead of escapism, the most suitable word would be rescue. In the postcolonial world, the change of "comfortable zone" made people lost themselves, but there were still ways to clear things up. Archie Belaney's masquerade was reasonable, he used his second identity to emphasize the worth and importance of native culture and propagandized the native cultures when so many whites treated Indianness only as a stumbling block to modern Western civilization.

3. Place: Where should I belong

A feature of all kinds of colonialism is the domination of place. What is one´s place? Place means not only simply space and location, this word in postcolonial system is a rather complex gather of language, history and environment and also accompanying emotional factors like a sense of displacement and alienation. In my opinion, the sense of displacement comes from migration, enslavement or alterity which may be put forward by similarities or differences between cultures. These feeling of alienation comes from a lost of 'comfortable zone' in language and place. The colonized people have been alienated from their homeland and their own language, tradition and culture through forced displacement. In this process, they experience a lost of naming as well. So when we work on the issues of cultural identity, place has been of great importance to postcolonial studies. How it becomes the horizon of identity?

3.1 Isabelle Eberhardt: Even the clearest mirror loses its function

Isabelle Eberhardt, an artist as a young nomad, is a case which is worth discussing.

> This Rimbaud-type woman repudiated Europe and its civilization, converted to Islam, dressed as a man, assumed a male identity, and roamed to Sahara, untrammeled by the constraints of her youth and sex.[6]

Isabelle Eberhardt is an intriguing figure, Her life was filled with "assumption". She treated herself as a man, she imagined her life as free and untrammeled. However, this kind of carnivalesque and relieved attitude was only in appearance. Paradoxically, she longed for a country, a place she could call her own, she wore a mask, on one hand, she persuaded herself that she was born to be a nomad and owned a free and racial soul, she tried to break free from the role that society and convention imposed on her gender without considering what other people thought. On the other hand, she never stopped searching a homeland, not only a house, but also a spiritual home. " I have given up," she wrote in her *Journaliers*, " the hope of ever having a corner on earth to call my own, a home, a family, peace or prosperity. " [7]Another example, Isabelle intended being a man and an Arab. But it showed also a contradictory situation. A man signifies the strong will to conquer, however, An Arab symbolized the conquered. These ambiguous situations in the public world produced a sense of displacement and alienation, what is apparent in every one of her writings.

She had written a narrative called „The Mirror", which we have discussed in the class. A mirror is a reflection, but what we see is the real of us or not? It's quite like a philosophical problem, but it could truely reflect the real situation of Eberhardt. The figure, who was made by Eberhardt, gazed attentively and seriously at himself for quite a long time, but he still wondered who he was. Whether he could know himself was not depend on the time he looked at himself in the mirror. It is the ambiguous life situation, which made him confused. Eberhardt put herself into this figure, I think, what she wants to say is that, The mirror should

---

[6] Abdel-Jaouad, Hedi, Isabelle Eberhardt: Portrait Of The Artist As A Young Nomad (1993). Yale University Press, No. 83,Volume 2. P..93
[7] Abdel-Jaouad, Hedi, Isabelle Eberhardt: Portrait Of The Artist As A Young Nomad (1993). Yale University Press, No.83. Volume2. P.106

have been a clear media, through this media we can clearly know ourselves, but for this kind of „non-identity" people like her, even the clearest mirror might lose its function.

"Writing through travel" is a feature of her works. Her nomadic writing seems like a long process, she was wandering from one language to another, experienced from one culture to another. Pierre Joris has ever said: "nomadic poetics is a war machine, always on the move, always changing, morphing, moving through languages, cultures, terrains, times without stopping."[8] In my opinion, her sense of non-belonging emerged during the travel. Such as, she grew up speaking and reading Russian, but used French as a way of communication. When she became a Muslim, Her language changed from "world language" to "a language of spiritual merit". It was like a drift from profane to sacred. So the imperialism causes a profoud language alienation. The writer had to shift their language to make it fit different kinds of circumstances and its new contexts.

We can find that her writings are unromantic, it is not similar to her life. She wrote exclusively about the dehumanizing effects of French colonial rules. Her homelessness sharpened her sense of responsibility to support humanity and speak for vulnerable groups.

We can draw a conclusion from the case of Isabelle Eberhardt, the place is not just a location, it reflects also the cultural memory and the feeling which were buried in the postcolonial world.

4. Grey Owl and Isabelle Eberhardt: a comparison

In this part, I want to put the word "ambiguity" as a key word. Both these two figures faced ambiguous conditions.

Eberhardt's ambiguity reflected in her writings. Her life and her texts have discrepancy. In her writings, she showed a conservative moral, it seemed that her novels was written by a traditional woman, In her texts, it is hard to find some unconventional parts that made you know her strong personality. But she was a cross-gender and cross-dressing woman with unconventional lifestyle. But can we say that her text was divorced from her life? The answer

---

[8] Joris, Pierre. (2003). A Nomad Poetics: Essays .Wesleyan University Press, P26.

is no. In fact, art originates from life, when she wrote her stories, she just tried to transform her life as a piece of fiction in which she presented changing roles, which can be seen through her different kinds of pseudonyms. She used this fictionalization of her life to reconcile herself with the world. Her life and her writings were not separated.

Grey Owl's ambiguity was showed in his masquerade. He was regarded as a fraud when people knew his parentage. But without doubt, he was the greatest pioneer spokesman for the Canadian wilderness. But in fact, it is not so exact by saying that he is a protector for Canada. His choice was not Canada, but "natural" Canada. What he wanted to protect is a part of Canada which was surrounded by endless forests, rivers and wilderness. When his masquerade was exposed, people may think it as difficult to judge which part in his writings is the truth and which part is the fiction. But we can't deny, he showed his love of the North, the animal. His benefits of his work has far outweighed the possible negative effects of his disguise. It was his impersonation that let him to gain a widespread fame and awake people a emotional awareness to protect the nature. He owned double identities, but all his identities are significative. It was just like a mirror, his identities saw each other through the mirror and knew what should they do to make a better life. So I want to put the word transformation here to say that sometimes such an ambiguous situation can also be transformed in a clear one.

5. Conclusion

In my essay, I tried to cover the problems such as identity, place and language in postcolonial world. Besides Grey Owl and Isabelle Eberhardt, a huge number of theorists and novelists also faced the problem of identity. The truth is that, once the individuals or societies were colonized, it became really difficult for them to find their true identities. Standing between past and present, their ambiguous conditions became obvious. They feel they detached from their previous culture and society and are still not able to fit the atmosphere of decolonization. The question of "Who am I" still exists even if the colonized countries gained independence.

References

1. Abdel-Jaouad, Hedi, Isabelle Eberhardt: Portrait Of The Artist As A Young Nomad (1993). Yale University Press No. 83.Volume 2
2. Ashcroft, Bill et al. (1989) *The Empire Writes Back: Theory and Practice in post-colonial literatures*. London-New York: Routledge
3. Hall, Stuart. (1990). 'Cultural Identity and Diaspora' in Jonathan Rutherford, *Identity:Community, Culture, Difference*, London:Lawrece and Wishart.
4. Hume, David. (2007). *A Treatise of Human Nature: Volume 1:Texts* Clarendon Press, Oxford
5. Joris, Pierre. (2003) *A Nomad Poetics: Essays*. Wesleyan University Press
6. Smith-Rosenberg, Carroll. (2010) *This Violent Empire – The Birth Of An American National Identity*. The University Of North Carolina Press, America
7. http://canadianicon.org/table-of-contents/grey-owl-white-indian/

YOUR KNOWLEDGE HAS VALUE

- We will publish your bachelor's and master's thesis, essays and papers

- Your own eBook and book - sold worldwide in all relevant shops

- Earn money with each sale

Upload your text at www.GRIN.com
and publish for free